T0063839

Bilingual WORDS
ANIMALS • ENGLISH – SPANISH
1000
ANIMALES • INGLÉS – ESPAÑOL
PALABRAS bilingües

DK | Penguin Random House

Written by Jules Pottle
US Senior Editor Shannon Beatty
Project Editor Robin Moul
Project Art Editor Vic Palastanga
Designed by Nidhi Mehra, Sadie Thomas, Nehal Verma
Design assistance Sif Nørskov
DTP Designer Dheeraj Singh, Syed Md Farhan
Picture Researchers Niharika Chauhan, Vagisha Pushp, Sakshi Saluja
Jacket Coordinator Issy Walsh
Senior Production Editor Nikoleta Parasaki
Senior Production Controller Ena Matagic
Managing Editor Penny Smith
Senior Managing Art Editor Romi Chakraborty
Deputy Art Director Mabel Chan
Publishing Director Sarah Larter

Spanish edition
Editorial Coordination Marina Alcione
Editorial Assistance and Production Eduard Sepúlveda

Editorial Services Tinta Simpàtica
Translation Anna Nualart

First American Edition, 2023
Published in the United States by DK Publishing
1745 Broadway, 20th Floor, New York, NY 10019
DK, a Division of Penguin Random House LLC

Original title: *1000 Animal Words*
First bilingual reprint: 2024
Copyright © 2023 Dorling Kindersley Limited
© Spanish translation 2023 Dorling Kindersley Limited

ISBN: 978-0-7440-8920-2

DK books are available at special discounts when purchased in bulk for sales promotions, premiums, fund-raising, or educational use. For details, contact: DK Publishing Special Markets, 1745 Broadway, 20th Floor, New York, NY 10019
SpecialSales@dk.com

Printed and bound in China

www.dkespañol.com

MIX
Paper | Supporting
responsible forestry
FSC™ C018179

This book was made with Forest Stewardship Council™ certified paper – one small step in DK's commitment to a sustainable future. For more information go to www.dk.com/our-green-pledge

Bilingual WORDS
ANIMALS • ENGLISH – SPANISH

1000

ANIMALES • INGLÉS – ESPAÑOL
PALABRAS bilingües

DK

A note for parents and carers
Nota para padres y cuidadores

What is an animal? If you ask a child, they are likely to name a pet or a farm animal. Many of them will be fluffy, or colorful, or have big eyes, like us. They are familiar. However, these are not the only animals that are important.

Some of the animals children encounter in their everyday lives may be considered pests, such as arachnids and insects. Others may be too small or too dull in color to catch a child's attention. But these seemingly insignificant, everyday animals are just as important to the balance of their ecosystem as the larger, more conspicuous species such as bears, elephants, or kangaroos.

It is fascinating to see how diverse the animal kingdom can be: from the brightly colored birds of the rainforest to the perfect camouflage of a stick insect. Every species plays a part in the delicate balance of our planet, so we need to appreciate the value of each and every one. And appreciation begins with knowledge and understanding.

Now, more than ever, we need to develop a respect for all animals and learn how to protect them. This bilingual book aims to nurture a curiosity and love for these animals in all the young readers. Explore the pages with children to learn together vocabulary in English and Spanish and to discuss the world around us and how we can take care of it for generations to come.

Jules Pottle
Primary science consultant, teacher, trainer, and author

¿Qué es un animal? Si lo preguntamos a un niño seguramente nos hablará de alguna mascota o un animal de granja. Muchos de ellos son peludos o coloridos, o tienen unos ojos grandes, como nosotros. Nos resultan familiares. Pero no son los únicos animales importantes.

Algunos de los animales que los niños ven en su vida cotidiana pueden considerarse plagas, como los arácnidos y los insectos. Otros pueden ser muy pequeños o tener un color demasiado apagado para llamar su atención. Pero estos animales cotidianos, insignificantes a primera vista, son tan importantes para sus ecosistemas como los más grandes y llamativos, como los osos, los elefantes o los canguros.

Es fascinante ver lo diverso que puede ser el reino animal: desde los pájaros de vivos colores de la selva tropical hasta el camuflaje perfecto de un insecto palo. Cada especie desempeña un papel en el delicado equilibrio de nuestro planeta, y por ello debemos apreciar el valor de todas y cada una de ellas. Y el aprecio comienza con el conocimiento y la comprensión.

Ahora más que nunca debemos tener respeto por todos los animales y aprender a protegerlos. El objetivo de este libro bilingüe es alimentar la curiosidad y el amor por estos animales en los jóvenes lectores. Explora sus páginas con los niños para aprender juntos vocabulario en inglés y español y para hablar sobre el mundo que nos rodea y sobre cómo podemos cuidarlo para las generaciones venideras.

Jules Pottle
Consultora de introducción a la ciencia, profesora, formadora y autora

Contents
Contenidos

Classifications
Clasificaciones

Animals are classified as vertebrates or invertebrates. Within those two groups there are smaller groups. Here are some of them.

Los animales se clasifican en vertebrados o invertebrados. En cada uno de estos dos grupos hay otros más pequeños. Estos son algunos.

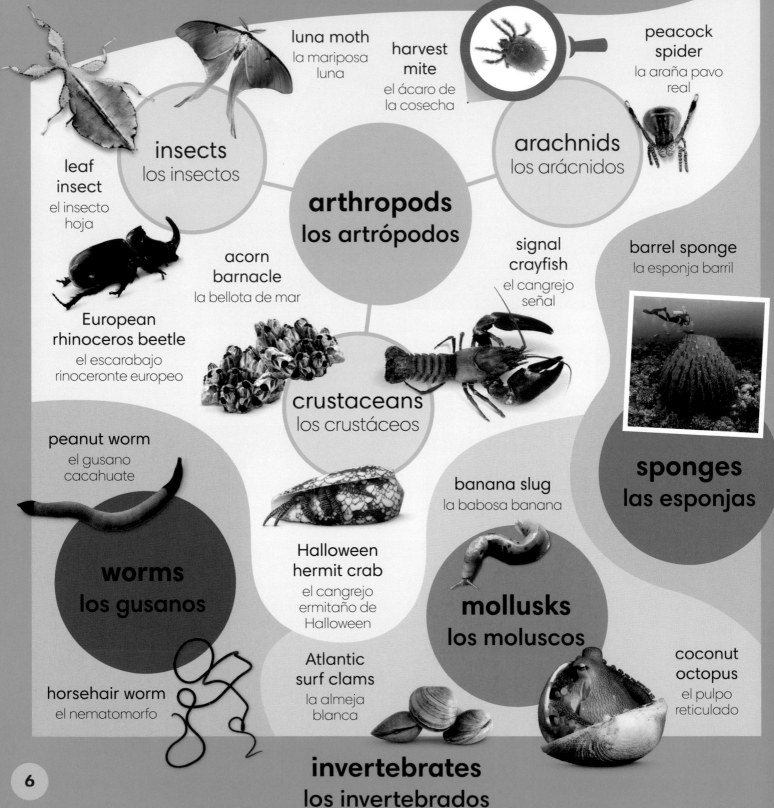

luna moth
la mariposa luna

harvest mite
el ácaro de la cosecha

peacock spider
la araña pavo real

insects
los insectos

arachnids
los arácnidos

leaf insect
el insecto hoja

arthropods
los artrópodos

signal crayfish
el cangrejo señal

barrel sponge
la esponja barril

acorn barnacle
la bellota de mar

European rhinoceros beetle
el escarabajo rinoceronte europeo

crustaceans
los crustáceos

sponges
las esponjas

peanut worm
el gusano cacahuate

banana slug
la babosa banana

worms
los gusanos

Halloween hermit crab
el cangrejo ermitaño de Halloween

mollusks
los moluscos

coconut octopus
el pulpo reticulado

horsehair worm
el nematomorfo

Atlantic surf clams
la almeja blanca

invertebrates
los invertebrados

cockatiel
la cacatúa
ninfa

birds
las aves

ring-billed gull
la gaviota de Delaware

Somali
giraffe
la jirafa
somalí

greater roadrunner
el correcaminos grande

quokka
el quokka

great
crested
newt
el tritón
crestado

golden
toad
el sapo
dorado

mammals
los mamíferos

amphibians
los anfibios

fire
salamander
la salamandra
común

gray whale
la ballena gris

fish
los peces

koi
la carpa
koi

reptiles
los reptiles

hawksbill
sea turtle
la tortuga carey

leopard
gecko
el gecko
leopardo

stingray
la raya

vertebrates
los vertebrados

7

Invertebrates
Los invertebrados

Most animal species are invertebrates with no internal bony skeleton.

La mayoría de las especies animales son invertebradas, sin esqueleto óseo interno.

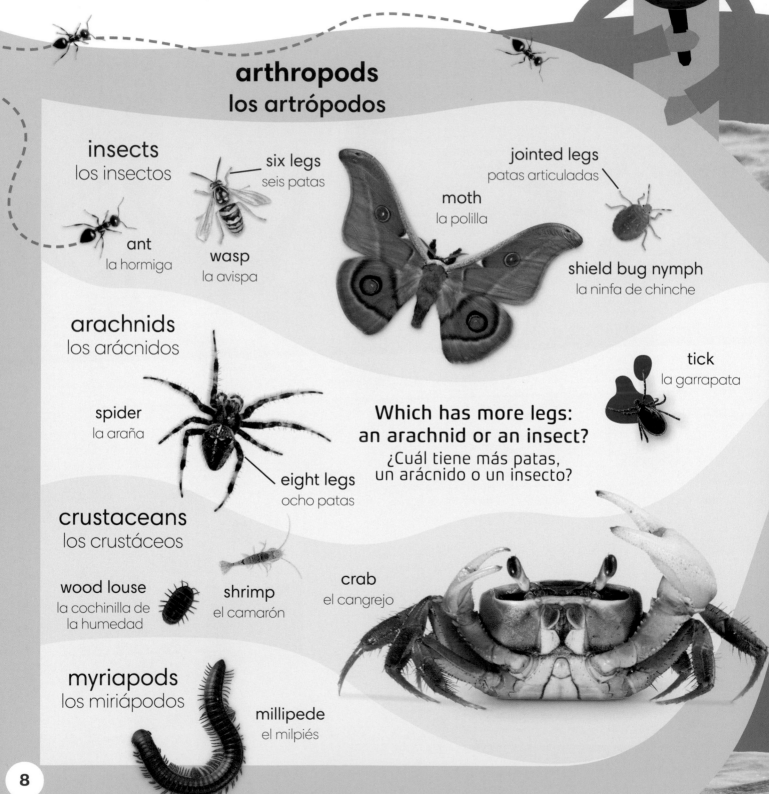

arthropods
los artrópodos

insects
los insectos

six legs
seis patas

ant
la hormiga

wasp
la avispa

moth
la polilla

jointed legs
patas articuladas

shield bug nymph
la ninfa de chinche

arachnids
los arácnidos

spider
la araña

eight legs
ocho patas

tick
la garrapata

Which has more legs: an arachnid or an insect?

¿Cuál tiene más patas, un arácnido o un insecto?

crustaceans
los crustáceos

wood louse
la cochinilla de la humedad

shrimp
el camarón

crab
el cangrejo

myriapods
los miriápodos

millipede
el milpiés

All invertebrates share these features.
Todos los invertebrados comparten las mismas características.

no bony skeleton
sin esqueleto óseo

cold-blooded
sangre fría

no spine
sin columna vertebral

lay eggs
ponen huevos

cuttlefish
la sepia

slug
la babosa

clam
la almeja

mollusks
los moluscos

starfish
la estrella de mar

tentacles
los tentáculos

octopus
el pulpo

brittle star
la ofiura

five legs
cinco patas

echinoderms
los equinodermos

sea cucumber
el pepino de mar

Pacific sea nettle
la ortiga del Pacífico

leech
la sanguijuela

jellyfish and corals
las medusas y los corales

sponges
las esponjas

hydrostatic skeleton
el hidroesqueleto

tree gorgonian coral
el coral blando

segmented worms
los anélidos

Can you think of some other invertebrates that live underwater?
¿Se te ocurren otros invertebrados que vivan bajo el agua?

Insects
Los insectos

There are more species of insects than any other type of animal on Earth.

En la Tierra hay más especies de insectos que de ningún otro tipo de animal.

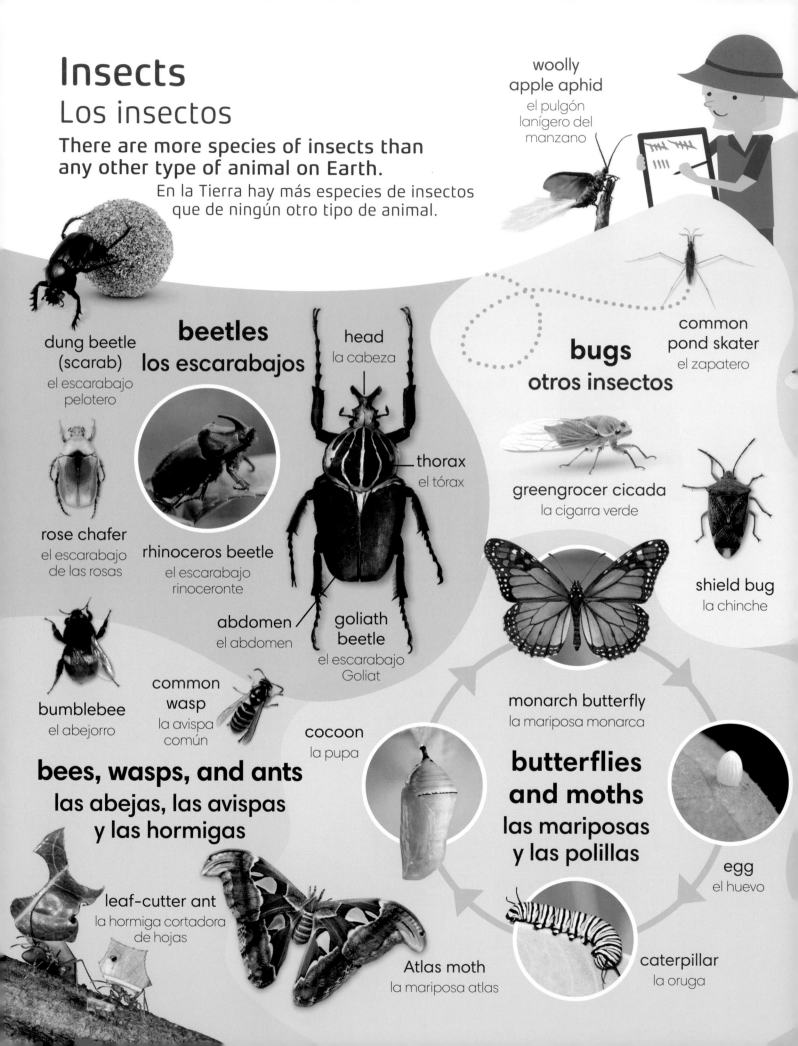

woolly apple aphid
el pulgón lanígero del manzano

beetles
los escarabajos

dung beetle (scarab)
el escarabajo pelotero

rose chafer
el escarabajo de las rosas

rhinoceros beetle
el escarabajo rinoceronte

head
la cabeza

thorax
el tórax

abdomen
el abdomen

goliath beetle
el escarabajo Goliat

bumblebee
el abejorro

common wasp
la avispa común

bees, wasps, and ants
las abejas, las avispas y las hormigas

leaf-cutter ant
la hormiga cortadora de hojas

cocoon
la pupa

Atlas moth
la mariposa atlas

bugs
otros insectos

common pond skater
el zapatero

greengrocer cicada
la cigarra verde

shield bug
la chinche

monarch butterfly
la mariposa monarca

butterflies and moths
las mariposas y las polillas

egg
el huevo

caterpillar
la oruga

common bluetail damselfly
el cola azul común

emperor dragonfly
la libélula emperador

desert locust
la langosta del desierto

crickets, locusts, and grasshoppers
los grillos, las langostas y los saltamontes

dragonflies and damselflies
las libélulas y los zigópteros

nymph
la ninfa

common field grasshopper
el saltamontes común

great green cricket
el saltamontes longicornio

termites
las termitas

cockroaches
las cucarachas

fleas
las pulgas

American cockroach
la cucaracha americana

globe skimmer dragonfly
la libélula rayadora naranja

hissing cockroach
la cucaracha silbadora

dog flea
la pulga de perro

termite
la termita

earwigs
las tijeretas

common mayfly
la efímera común

mayflies
las efímeras

European earwig
la tijereta europea

praying mantises
las mantis religiosas

stick insects and leaf insects
los insectos palo y los insectos hoja

leaf insect
el insecto hoja

Mediterranean praying mantis
la mantis mediterránea

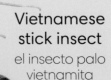

Vietnamese stick insect
el insecto palo vietnamita

Birds
Las aves

Birds have beaks and feathers. They lay eggs with hard shells. Birds that fly have hollow bones to make them lighter.

Las aves tienen pico y plumas y ponen huevos de cáscara dura. Los huesos de las aves que vuelan están huecos y eso las hace más ligeras.

birds of prey
las aves de presa

osprey
el águila pescadora

sparrow hawk
el gavilán

barn owl
la lechuza común

seabirds
las aves marinas

wandering albatross
el albatros viajero

masked booby
el piquero enmascarado

Atlantic puffin
el frailecillo común

common gull
la gaviota común

waterbirds
las aves acuáticas

Which birds are native to where you live?

¿Qué aves son nativas de donde vives tú?

mute swan
el cisne mudo

wading birds
las aves zancudas

greater flamingo
el flamenco común

yellow-billed stork
el tántalo africano

mallard duck
el pato real

Canada goose
el ganso de Canadá

All birds share these features.
Todas las aves comparten las mismas características.

bony skeleton
esqueleto óseo

warm-blooded
sangre caliente

hard-shelled eggs
huevos de cáscara dura

feathers
plumas

scaly legs
patas escamosas

flightless birds
las aves no voladoras

bald eagle
el águila calva

common ostrich
el avestruz

emu
el emú

kiwi
el kiwi

penguins
los pingüinos

emperor penguin
el pingüino emperador

gentoo penguin
el pingüino juanito

domestic birds
las aves domésticas

chicken
el pollo

small birds
las aves pequeñas

common wood pigeon
la paloma torcaz

common swift
el vencejo común

blue tit
el herrerillo común

house sparrow
el gorrión común

parrots
los loros

galah
la cacatúa Galah

scarlet macaw
el guacamayo escarlata

ruby-throated hummingbird
el colibrí de garganta roja

European robin
el petirrojo europeo

13

Amphibians
Los anfibios

Most amphibians live on land for much of the year. They must return to water to breed because their eggs have no shells.

La mayoría de los anfibios viven en tierra buena parte del año. Deben volver al agua para criar, puesto que sus huevos no tienen cáscara.

frogs and toads
las ranas y los sapos

salamanders
las salamandras

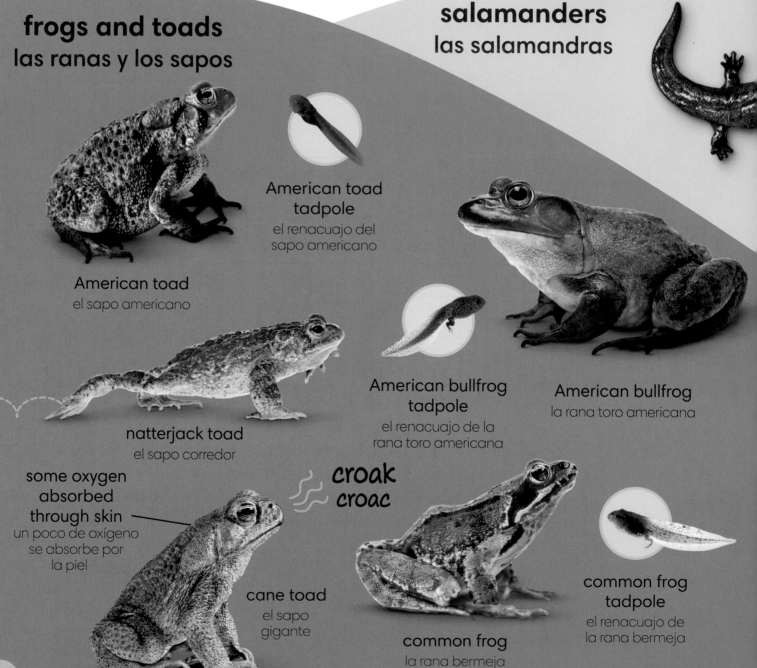

American toad tadpole
el renacuajo del sapo americano

American toad
el sapo americano

American bullfrog tadpole
el renacuajo de la rana toro americana

American bullfrog
la rana toro americana

natterjack toad
el sapo corredor

some oxygen absorbed through skin
un poco de oxígeno se absorbe por la piel

croak
croac

cane toad
el sapo gigante

common frog
la rana bermeja

common frog tadpole
el renacuajo de la rana bermeja

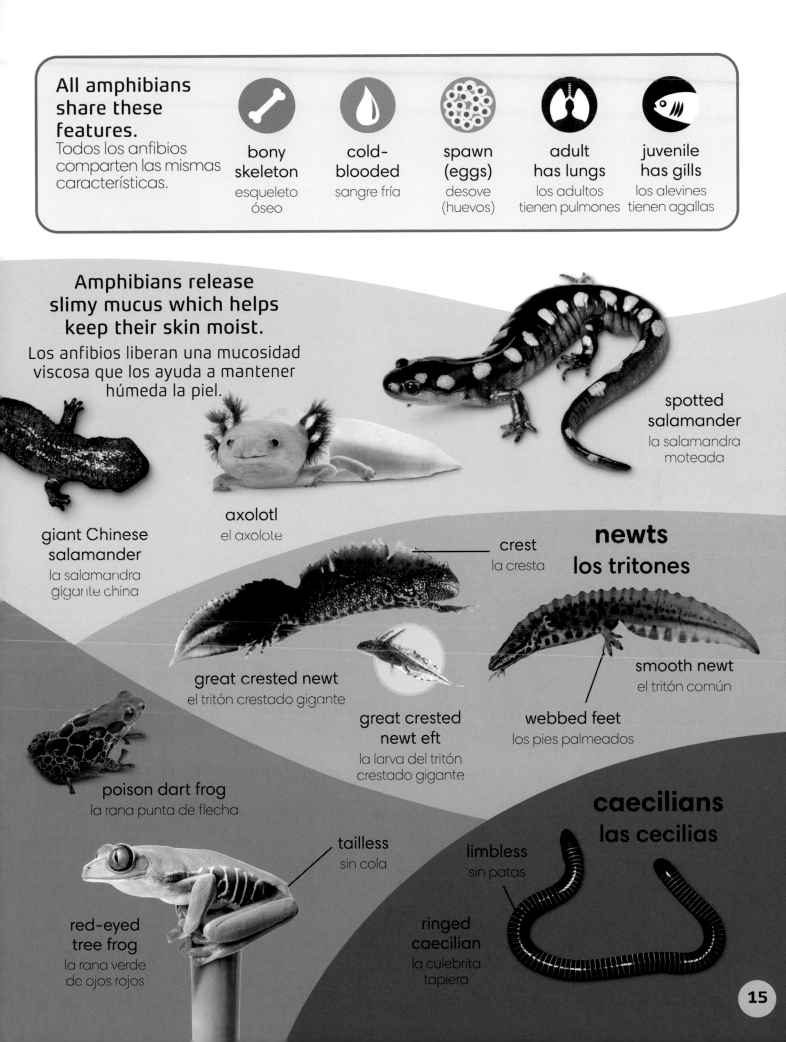

All amphibians share these features.
Todos los anfibios comparten las mismas características.

bony skeleton
esqueleto óseo

cold-blooded
sangre fría

spawn (eggs)
desove (huevos)

adult has lungs
los adultos tienen pulmones

juvenile has gills
los alevines tienen agallas

Amphibians release slimy mucus which helps keep their skin moist.
Los anfibios liberan una mucosidad viscosa que los ayuda a mantener húmeda la piel.

spotted salamander
la salamandra moteada

axolotl
el axolote

giant Chinese salamander
la salamandra gigante china

crest
la cresta

newts
los tritones

great crested newt
el tritón crestado gigante

great crested newt eft
la larva del tritón crestado gigante

smooth newt
el tritón común

webbed feet
los pies palmeados

poison dart frog
la rana punta de flecha

tailless
sin cola

limbless
sin patas

caecilians
las cecilias

red-eyed tree frog
la rana verde de ojos rojos

ringed caecilian
la culebrita tapiera

15

Mammals
Los mamíferos

Mammals give birth to live young, which feed on their mother's milk.
Los mamíferos dan a luz crías vivas, que se alimentan de la leche de su madre.

All mammals share these features.
Todos los mamíferos comparten las mismas características.

Bactrian camel
el camello bactriano

brown-throated sloth
el perezoso bayo

bonnet macaque
el macaco coronado

mongoose lemur
el lémur mangosta

mouse
el ratón

llama
la llama

Burchell's zebra
la cebra de Burchell

African elephant
el elefante africano

Some mammals, such as whales and dolphins, live underwater.
Algunos mamíferos, como las ballenas y los delfines, viven bajo el agua.

North American river otter
la nutria de río de América del Norte

bottlenose dolphin
el delfín nariz de botella

sperm whale
el cachalote

16

pangolin
el pangolín

bat
el murciélago

ermine
el armiño

red panda
el panda rojo

capybara
el capibara

sun bear
el oso malayo

brown hare
la liebre común

warthog
el jabalí verrugoso

Virginia opossum
la zarigüeya de Virginia

marsupials
los marsupiales

ringed seal
la foca ocelada

wombat
el wómbat

wallaby
el ualabí

North America
América del Norte

New Guinea
Nueva Guinea

South America
América del Sur

koala
el koala

Australia
Australia

Tasmania
Tasmania

undeveloped young
la cría inmadura

monotremes
los monotremas

lays eggs
pone huevos

New Guinea
Nueva Guinea

Australia
Australia

echidna
el equidna

duck-billed platypus
el ornitorrinco

17

Primates
Los primates

Humans belong to the primate family. Our brains are highly complex, just like other primates.

Los humanos pertenecemos a la familia de los primates. Nuestro cerebro es muy complejo, igual que el de otros primates.

howler monkey
el mono aullador

grasp
agarra

golden lion tamarin
el tamarino león dorado

emperor tamarin
el tití emperador

woolly spider monkey
el mono araña lanudo

spider monkey
el mono araña

Monkey tails can grip branches, like an extra hand.

Los monos pueden agarrarse con la cola a las ramas, como si fuera una mano más.

swing through trees
se balancea en los árboles

use tools
utilizan herramientas

squirrel monkey
el mono ardilla

capuchin monkey
el mono capuchino

woolly monkey
el mono lanudo

titi
el tití

gibbon
el gibón

olive baboon
el papión oliva

vervet monkey
el cercopiteco verde

ring-tailed lemur
el lémur de cola anillada

aye-aye
el aye-aye

Abyssinian black-and-white colobus (guereza)
el colobo blanco y negro de Abisinia (guereza)

rhesus monkey
el macaco Rhesus

Barbary macaque
el macaco de Berbería

loris
el loris

talk
habla

human
la humana

gorilla
el gorila

bonobo
el bonobo

chimpanzee
el chimpancé

proboscis monkey
el mono narigudo

orangutan
el orangután

no tail
sin cola

19

Fish
Los peces

There are two types of fish. One type has a skeleton made of bone. The other has a skeleton made of cartilage, which is more flexible.

Existen dos tipos de peces, un tipo tiene el esqueleto formado por huesos o espinas, y el otro, por cartílago, que es más flexible.

All fish share these features.

Todos los peces comparten las mismas características.

cold-blooded
sangre fría

longsnout seahorse
el caballito de mar mediterráneo

freshwater angelfish
el pez ángel

batfish
el pez murciélago de cara roja

Atlantic salmon
el salmón del Atlántico

coelacanth
el celacanto

Atlantic bluefin tuna
el atún rojo del Atlántico

blue regal tang
el pez cirujano azul

puffer fish
el pez globo

clown fish
el pez payaso

electric eel
la anguila eléctrica

European plaice
la platija

anglerfish
el rape

blue catfish
el bagre azul

bony fish
los peces óseos

20

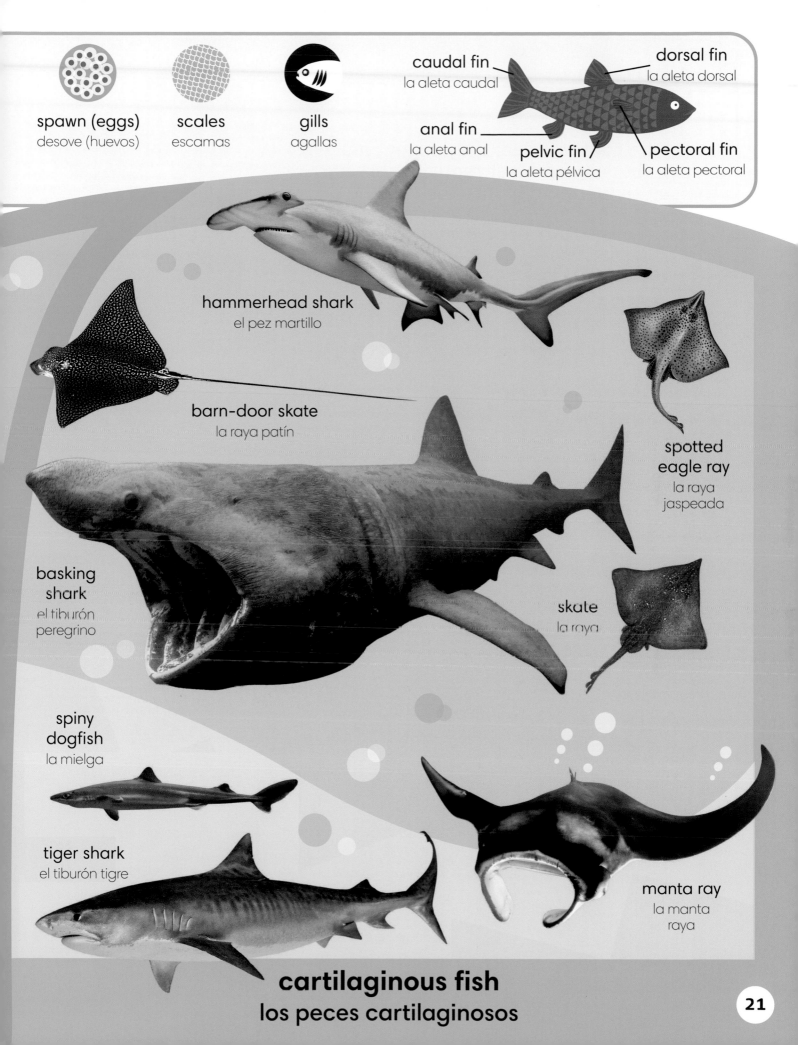

spawn (eggs)
desove (huevos)

scales
escamas

gills
agallas

caudal fin
la aleta caudal

dorsal fin
la aleta dorsal

anal fin
la aleta anal

pelvic fin
la aleta pélvica

pectoral fin
la aleta pectoral

hammerhead shark
el pez martillo

barn-door skate
la raya patín

spotted
eagle ray
la raya
jaspeada

basking
shark
el tiburón
peregrino

skate
la raya

spiny
dogfish
la mielga

tiger shark
el tiburón tigre

manta ray
la manta
raya

cartilaginous fish
los peces cartilaginosos

Reptiles
Los reptiles

Reptiles are cold-blooded: they cannot make their own body heat. Most reptiles must bask in the sun to warm up before they can be active.

Los reptiles tienen la sangre fría: no pueden producir su propio calor corporal. La mayoría de los reptiles deben ponerse al sol para calentarse antes de poder estar activos.

lizards
los lagartos

panther chameleon
el camaleón pantera

leopard gecko
el gecko leopardo

Komodo dragon
el dragón de Komodo

green Iguana
la iguana verde

Reptiles have been around for over 300 million years.

Los reptiles existen desde hace más de 300 millones de años.

diamondback terrapin
tortuga espalda de diamante

tortoises and turtles
las tortugas de agua y de tierra

crawl
se arrastran

shell (carapace)
el caparazón

scute
el escudo

Blanding's turtle
la tortuga Blandingii

red-footed tortoise
la tortuga terrestre de patas rojas

horny beak
el pico córneo

leg
la pata

Galapagos giant tortoise
la tortuga gigante de las Galápagos

claw
la garra

All reptiles share these features.
Todos los reptiles comparten las mismas características.

bony skeleton
esqueleto óseo

cold-blooded
sangre fría

leathery eggs
huevos correosos

scales
escamas

black mamba
la mamba negra

snakes
las serpientes

boa constrictor
la boa constrictor

sheds skin
mudan la piel

slither
se deslizan

fangs
los colmillos

forked tongue
la lengua bífida

tuataras
los tuátaras

tuatara
el tuátara

only in New Zealand
solo en Nueva Zelanda

tail ridge
la cola crestada

crocodiles and alligators
los cocodrilos y los caimanes

belly crawl
reptan

Nile crocodile
el cocodrilo del Nilo

American alligator
el caimán americano

webbed feet
los pies palmeados

Our pets
Nuestras mascotas

Humans enjoy the company of animals. We keep many different types of animals as pets.

Los humanos disfrutamos de la compañía de los animales. Tenemos muchos tipos de animales como mascotas.

terrapin
la tortuga de agua

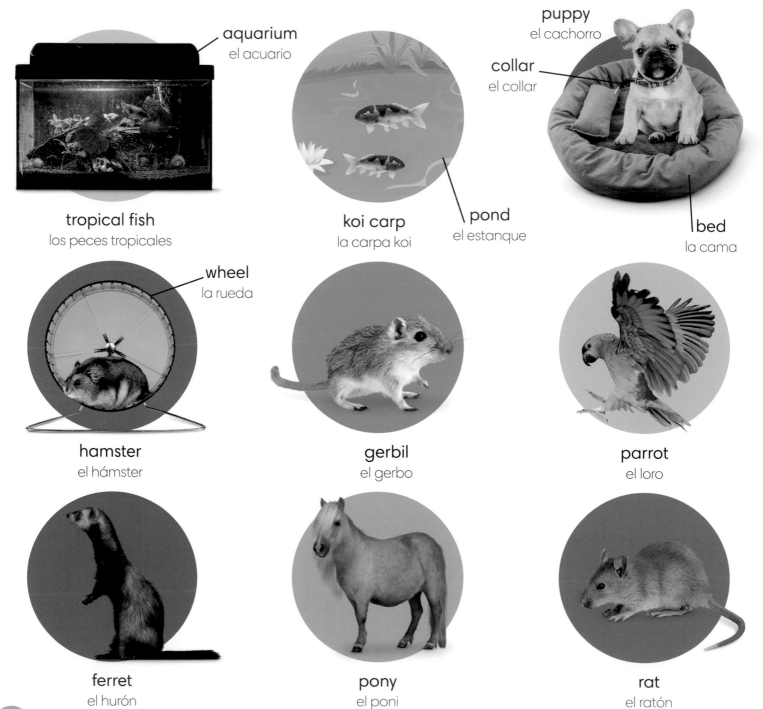

aquarium
el acuario

tropical fish
los peces tropicales

koi carp
la carpa koi

pond
el estanque

puppy
el cachorro

collar
el collar

bed
la cama

wheel
la rueda

hamster
el hámster

gerbil
el gerbo

parrot
el loro

ferret
el hurón

pony
el poni

rat
el ratón

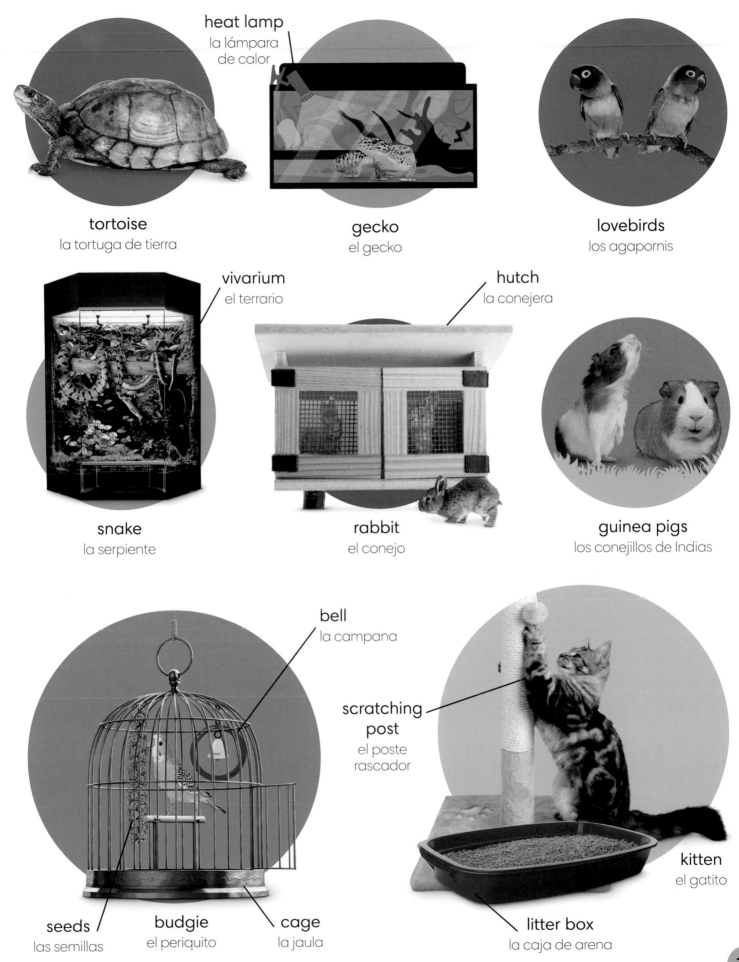

heat lamp
la lámpara
de calor

tortoise
la tortuga de tierra

gecko
el gecko

lovebirds
los agapornis

vivarium
el terrario

hutch
la conejera

snake
la serpiente

rabbit
el conejo

guinea pigs
los conejillos de Indias

bell
la campana

**scratching
post**
el poste
rascador

seeds
las semillas

budgie
el periquito

cage
la jaula

litter box
la caja de arena

kitten
el gatito

Domestic dogs
Los perros domésticos

Humans have kept dogs for thousands of years. Many breeds are working dogs. Others are bred to be good company.

Los humanos han tenido perros durante miles de años. Muchas razas son perros de trabajo. Otras se crían para ser una buena compañía.

> **Do you have a favorite dog breed?**
> ¿Hay alguna raza de perro que sea tu favorita?

hounds
los sabuesos

basset hound
el basset hound

beagle
el beagle

Irish wolfhound
el lebrel irlandés

whippet
el whippet

greyhound
el galgo

retrievers
los perros de caza

dachshund
el teckel

Irish setter
el setter irlandés

Norwegian elkhound
el cazador de alces noruego

cocker spaniel
el cocker spaniel

Labrador retriever
el labrador

golden retriever
el golden retriever

herding dogs
los perros pastores

Newfoundland
el terranova

boxer
el boxer

Samoyed
el samoyedo

Siberian husky
el husky siberiano

German shepherd
el pastor alemán

Old English sheepdog
el bobtail, antiguo pastor inglés

border collie
el border collie

Doberman pinscher
el dóberman

utility dogs
los perros de servicio

Yorkshire terrier
el Yorkshire terrier

Jack Russell
el Jack Russell terrier

toy dogs
los perros miniatura

Chihuahua
el chihuahua

French bulldog
el bulldog francés

toy poodle
el canicho

lapdogs
los perros falderos

shih tzu
el shih tzu

pug
el pug

cockapoo
el cockapoo

Cavalier King Charles spaniel
el Cavalier King Charles spaniel

Pekingese
el pequinés

Cats of all sizes
Felinos de todos los tamaños

Although they come in lots of different sizes, they share many of the same characteristics, including domestic cats.

Aunque los hay de muchos tamaños distintos, comparten muchas de las mismas características, incluso los gatos domésticos.

lynx
el lince

pampas cat
el gato de las pampas

jaguar
el jaguar

ocelot
el ocelote

leopard
el leopardo

puma
el puma

marbled cat
el gato jaspeado

Do you have a favorite cat species?
¿Hay alguna especie de felino que sea tu favorita?

feline features
las características felinas

hunters
cazadores

carnivorous
carnívoros

curved claws
garras curvas

cheetah
el guepardo

caracal
el caracal

sand cat
el gato del desierto

serval
el serval

Pallas's cat
el manul

snow leopard
el leopardo de las nieves

domestic cat breeds
las razas de gato doméstico

domestic shorthair
el doméstico de pelo corto

Himalayan
el himalayo

Maine coon
el Maine Coon

Siamese
el siamés

jaguarundi
el yaguarundí

long canine teeth
largos dientes caninos

carnassial teeth
muelas carniceras

whiskers
bigotes

night vision
visión nocturna

Animal sounds
Los sonidos de los animales

Animals make noises for many reasons. Different sounds help them communicate with family, scare away predators, and attract mates.

Los animales emiten sonidos por muchos motivos. Distintos sonidos los ayudan a comunicarse con su familia, ahuyentar a los depredadores o atraer a posibles parejas.

Habitats sound different because of the animals that live there.
En cada hábitat se oyen sonidos distintos por los animales que viven allí.

ocean
el océano

dolphins
los delfines

click
clic

whistle
silbido

orca
la orca

countryside
el campo

chirp
gorjeo

nuthatch
la sita

screech
chirrido

barn owl
la lechuza común

hoot hoot
uuuh uuuh

bark
ladrido

fox
el zorro

scream
aullido

tawny owl
el cárabo

squeak
chillido

peck peck
pic, pic

mouse
el ratón

croak
croac

woodpecker
el pájaro carpintero

frog
la rana

savannah
la sabana

chatter
parloteo

vervet monkey
el cercopiteco verde

trumpet
barrito

elephant
el elefante

rattle
vibración

hiss
silbido

snake
la serpiente

snarl
gruñido

roar
rugido

growl
grrr

lion
el león

farmyard
la granja

snort
gruñido

oink
oinc

pig
el cerdo

moo
muuu

cow
la vaca

bray
rebuzno

whinny
relincho

hee-haw
iii aaah

neigh
rebufo

donkey
el asno

nicker
patea

horse
el caballo

gobble gobble
glu glu

turkey
el pavo

baaa
beeee

bleat
balido

sheep
la oveja

quack
cuac

hiss
graznido

honk
onc

goose
el ganso

duck
el pato

cock-a-doodle-doo
quiquiriquí

cluck
clocó

chicken
el pollo

backyard
el jardín

coo
gru

pigeon
la paloma

woof
guau

bark
ladrido

dog
el perro

meow
miau

cat
el gato

buzz
bzzz

bees
las abejas

Superpowers
Los superpoderes

Some animals have abilities that are so incredible, they seem like superpowers!

¡Algunos animales tienen cualidades tan increíbles que parecen superpoderes!

firefly
la luciérnaga

bioluminescent
bioluminescente

tardigrade
el tardígrado

little brown bat
el pequeño murciélago café

**using ultrasound
usar ultrasonidos**

runs as fast as a car
corre tanto como un coche

hears sound too high for human ears
oye sonidos demasiado agudos para el oído humano

cheetah
el guepardo

suspended animation (pausing life)
animación suspendida (pone la vida en pausa)

plumed basilisk
el basilisco verde

runs on water
corre sobre el agua

electric eel
anguila eléctrica

salmon
el salmón

gives an electric shock
da descargas eléctricas

navigates long distances
nada largas distancias

the most venomous sting
el aguijón más venenoso

**intelligent
inteligente**

**flexible
flexible**

firefly squid
el calamar luciérnaga

escapes traps
escapa de las trampas

octopus
el pulpo

glows in the dark
brilla en la oscuridad

box jellyfish
la cubomedusa

the
fastest animal
el animal más
rápido

gecko
el gecko

walks
on ceiling
camina por
el techo

peregrine falcon
el halcón peregrino

quick dive
se zambulle
con rapidez

sticky toe pads
las almohadillas
adhesivas

amazing
sense of smell
olfato increíble

the most
venomous bite
la picadura más
venenosa

climbs
up walls
sube por las
paredes

jumping
saltar

funnel
web spider
la araña
de tela de
embudo

cat flea
la pulga
de gato

Alpine ibex
el íbice alpino

leaps 150 times
its body length
salta 150 veces su
longitud corporal

great
balance
gran equilibrio

silvertip grizzly bear
el oso gris

punches faster
than a bullet
el golpe de su
puño es
más veloz que
una bala

peacock mantis shrimp
el camarón mantis pavo real

On the move
En marcha

Animals move in different ways to get around, escape predators, or hunt prey.

Los animales se mueven de formas distintas para desplazarse, huir de los depredadores o cazar a sus presas.

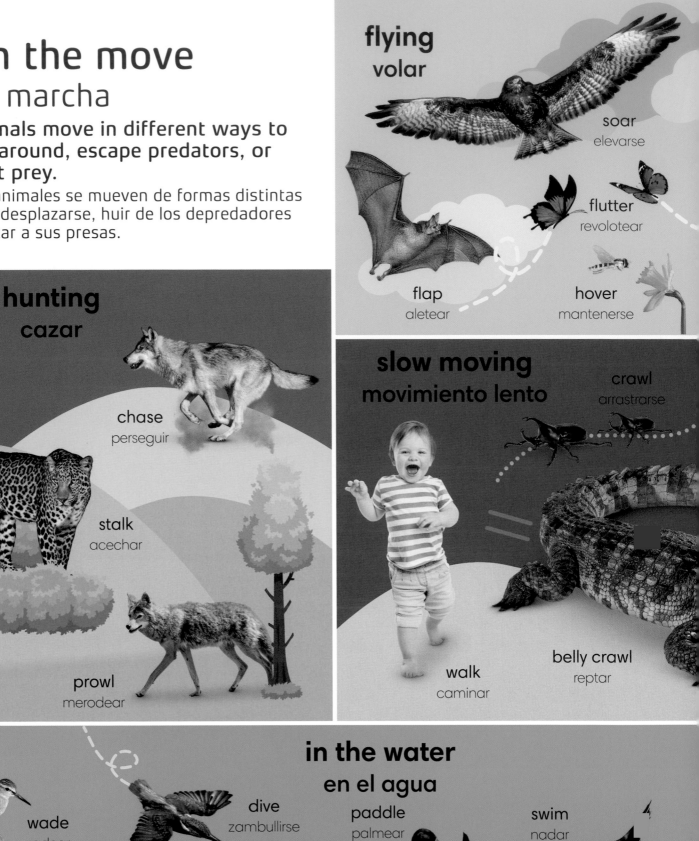

flying
volar

soar
elevarse

flutter
revolotear

flap
aletear

hover
mantenerse

hunting
cazar

chase
perseguir

stalk
acechar

prowl
merodear

slow moving
movimiento lento

crawl
arrastrarse

walk
caminar

belly crawl
reptar

in the water
en el agua

wade
vadear

dive
zambullirse

paddle
palmear

swim
nadar

squirt
propulsarse
a chorro

active flight
el vuelo activo

glide
planear

loop
ondularse

float
flotar

quick movements
movimientos rápidos

jump
saltar

gallop
galopar

hop
brincar

run
correr

in the trees
en los árboles

swing
balancearse

climb
trepar

unusual movements
movimientos poco usuales

knuckle walk
caminar sobre los nudillos

roll
hacer rodar

sidewind
reptan de lado

underground
bajo tierra

burrow
esconderse

wriggle
retorcerse

dig
cavar

35

Unusual animals
Los animales insólitos

**There are a wide variety of animals.
Some don't look like animals at all!**

Los animales son muy variados. Hay algunos
que ¡ni siquiera parece que sean animales!

saiga antelope
el saiga

pink fairy armadillo
el pichiciego

star-
nosed mole
el topo de
nariz
estrellada

northern
three-toed
jerboa
el jerbo de pies
peludos

matamata
sea turtle
la tortuga
matamata

thorny devil
el diablo espinoso

satanic leaf-tailed gecko
el gecko cola de hoja satánico

warty
frogfish
el pez rana
verrugoso

vase sponge
la esponja vítrea

sea pig
el cerdo
de mar

glass
sponge
la esponja
de cristal

brain coral
el coral
cerebro

purple sea pen
la pluma marina

mushroom
coral
el coral hongo

limpet
la lapa

Honduran white bat
el murciélago blanco hondureño

magnificent frigate bird
la fragata común

Indian purple frog
la rana púrpura

greater lophorina
el ave del paraíso soberbia

hummingbird hawk moth
la esfinge colibrí

Japanese emperor caterpillar
la oruga de la mariposa emperador japonés

dumbo octopus
el pulpo dumbo

red-lipped batfish
el pez murciélago de labios rojos

blue dragon sea slug
el dragón azul

firework jellyfish
la medusa de fuegos artificiales

macropinna microstoma
el pez cabeza transparente

blobfish
el cabeza gorda

barnacle
el percebe

leafy sea dragon
el dragón de mar foliado

sea bunny
el conejo de mar

goblin shark
el tiburón duende

Venus fan
la gorgonia

Colorful animals
Los animales coloridos

Vibrant colors often have a purpose in the animal kingdom, such as warnings, camouflage, and showing off!

Los colores llamativos a menudo tienen una razón de ser en el reino animal, ya sea para alertar, para camuflarse o para exhibirse.

"I'm pink because of the food I eat!"
"¡Soy de color rosa a causa de lo que como!".

flamingo
el flamenco

neon tetra
el tetra neón

freshwater angelfish
el pez ángel

keel-billed toucan
el tucán pico iris

scarlet macaw
el guacamayo escarlata

"My bright colors help me attract a mate."
"Mis vivos colores me ayudan a atraer una pareja".

crowntail betta
el pez betta

fiery throated hummingbird
el colibrí insigne

golden snub-nosed monkey
el langur chato dorado

Moorish idol
el ídolo moro

Indian peafowl
el pavo real

green discus
el pez disco

candy basslet
el lipropoma

oriental dwarf kingfisher
el martín pescador oriental

Wilson's bird-of-paradise
el ave del paraíso republicana

boomslang snake
la culebra arborícola de El Cabo

orchid mantis
la mantis orquídea

"My color helps me hide among flowers."
"Mi color me ayuda a camuflarme entre las flores".

blue morpho
la morfo azul

Indonesian pit viper
la serpiente azul de Indonesia

peacock spider
la araña pavo real

eastern box turtle
la tortuga de caja oriental

panther chameleon
el camaloón pantera

red lionfish
el pez león colorado

"My color warns other animals that I'm poisonous."
"Mi color avisa a otros animales de que soy venenoso".

crowned jellyfish
la medusa coronada

peacock mantis shrimp
camarón mantis pavo real

blue dart frog
la rana flecha azul

jewel beetle
el escarabajo joya

Picasso bug
la chinche Picasso

rose maple moth
la polilla del arce rosa

mandrill
el mandril

beadlet anemone
el tomate de mar

Royal gramma
el pez abuela real

golden tortoise beetle
el escarabajo tortuga dorada

rainbow parrotfish
el pez loro guacamayo

blue-ringed octopus
el pulpo de anillos azules

Camouflage
El camuflaje

Camouflage helps animals blend in with their habitats and stay hidden from view.

El camuflaje ayuda a los animales a esconderse en su hábitat.

look like snow
parecen nieve

white-tailed ptarmigan
el lagópodo coliblanco

Arctic fox
el zorro ártico

Arctic
el Ártico

look like bark and leaves
parecen corteza y hojas

peppered moth
la mariposa de los abedules

copperhead snake
la serpiente cabeza de cobre

great horned owl
el búho americano

long-eared owl
el búho chico

boreal forest
el bosque boreal

look like plants
parecen plantas

mossy leaf-tail gecko
el *Uroplatus sikorae*

ghost mantis
la mantis de hoja muerta

walking stick
el insecto palo

common potoo
el nictibio urutaú

tropical forest
el bosque tropical

Eastern chipmunk
la ardilla listada del Este americano

red squirrel
la ardilla roja

mountain caribou
el caribú

temperate forest
el bosque templado

look like dappled shade
parecen sombras moteadas

spotted hyena
la hiena manchada

impala
el impala

leopard
el leopardo

African wild dog
el licaón

savanna
la sabana

blue shark
la tintorera

hard to see from above and below
difícil de ver desde arriba y desde abajo

looks like seafloor
parece el fondo marino

stone flounder
el *Kareius bicoloratus*

underwater
bajo el agua

look like flowers
parecen flores

goldenrod crab spider
la araña cangrejo

orchid mantis
la mantis orquídea

flowers
las flores

nightjar
el chotacabras

looks like the ground
parece el suelo

mugger crocodile
el cocodrilo de las marismas

looks like a log
parece un tronco

riverbank
la ribera

Home sweet home
Hogar, dulce hogar

There are all kinds of homes in the animal kingdom. Some animals build their own home, while others find existing spots to settle in.

En el reino animal hay toda clase de casas. Algunos animales construyen su propio hogar, mientras que otros buscan el rincón adecuado para instalarse.

bat
el murciélago
roost
el dormidero

bear
el oso
den
la guarida

wild boar
el jabalí
temporary nest
el nido temporal

prairie dog
el perrito de las praderas
town
la colonia

harvest mouse
el ratón de los cultivos
nest in stalks
el nido en los tallos

red squirrel
la ardilla roja
nest (drey)
el nido

otter
la nutria
holt
la guarida

beaver
el castor
lodge inside a dam
la madriguera en un dique

fox
el zorro
earth
la guarida

rabbit
el conejo
warren
la madriguera

water vole
el topillo de agua
burrow
la madriguera

badger
el tejón
sett
la guarida

sociable weaverbird
el tejedor republicano
multistory nest
el nido de varios niveles

baya weaverbird
el tejedor baya
nest colony
el nido colonia

rufous hornero
el hornero común
clay nest
el nido de barro

golden eagle
el águila real
aerie
la aguilera

clown fish
el pez payaso
anemone
la anémona

limpet
la lapa
rock
la roca

hanging nests
los nidos colgantes

Montezuma oropendola
la oropéndola de Moctezuma
pendulous nest
el nido colgante

nest with hexagonal cells
los nidos con celdas hexagonales

paper wasp
la avispa papelera europea
nest
el nido

Australian leaf-curling spider
la araña deformadora de hojas
leaf
la hoja

curls a leaf to make a home
curva una hoja para hacerse un hogar

froghopper
la chicharrita
cuckoo spit
el mucílago

European red wood ant
la hormiga roja europea
anthill
el hormiguero

tent moth
la oruga de tienda
tent made of silk
la tienda hecha de seda

leaves woven together
las hojas cosidas entre sí

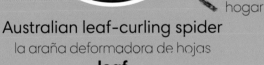

Australian weaver ants
las hormigas tejedoras australianas
nest made of leaves
el nido hecho de hojas

Baby animals
Las crías de los animales

Animals change as they grow up. Some change completely, others just grow bigger.

Los animales cambian a medida que crecen. Algunos cambian por completo y otros, simplemente, crecen.

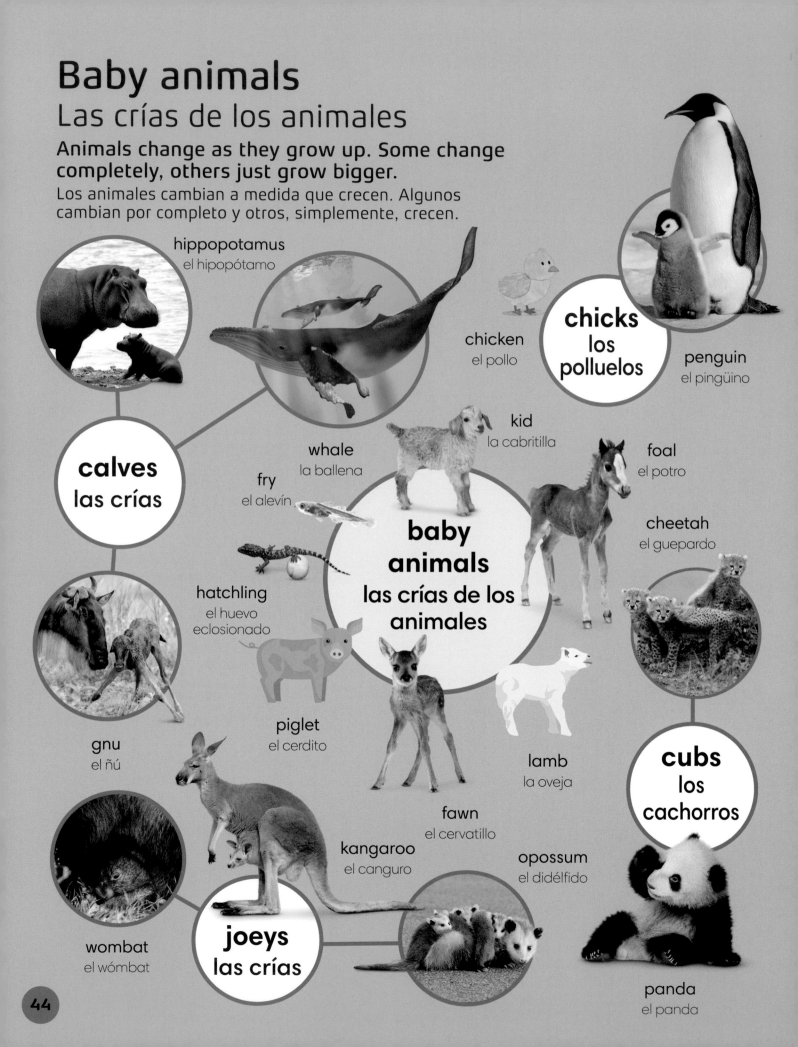

hippopotamus
el hipopótamo

chicken
el pollo

chicks
los
polluelos

penguin
el pingüino

whale
la ballena

kid
la cabritilla

foal
el potro

calves
las crías

fry
el alevín

cheetah
el guepardo

**baby
animals**
las crías de los
animales

hatchling
el huevo
eclosionado

gnu
el ñú

piglet
el cerdito

lamb
la oveja

cubs
los
cachorros

kangaroo
el canguro

fawn
el cervatillo

opossum
el didélfido

wombat
el wómbat

joeys
las crías

panda
el panda

green sea turtle
la tortuga verde

reptiles, fish,
birds: egg laying
los reptiles, los peces,
las aves: ponen huevos

laying eggs
ponen huevos

pit in
sand
el hoyo en
la arena

otter
la nutria

mammals:
live young
los mamíferos:
crías vivas

pup
el cachorro

live birth
nacen vivas

frog
la rana

froglet
la ranita

adult frog
la rana adulta

amphibian:
metamorphosis
los anfibios:
la metamorfosis

tadpole
el renacuajo

spawn
el desove

spurge hawk-moth
la esfinge de la lechetrezna

pupa
la pupa

adult
el adulto

insect
complete
metamorphosis
metamorfosis
completa de
un insecto

larva
la larva

egg
el huevo

green shield bug
la chinche

later
nymph
la ninfa

adult
adult

insect
incomplete
metamorphosis
metamorfosis
incompleta
de un insecto

young nymph
la ninfa joven

eggs
los huevos

45

Eggs of all kinds
Huevos de todo tipo

Fish eggs, bird eggs, turtle eggs, insect eggs—they all look different.

Huevos de pez, huevos de ave, huevos de tortuga, huevos de insecto... todos son distintos.

bird eggs
los huevos de las aves

ostrich
de avestruz

melodious warbler
de zarcero común

vervain hummingbird
de colibrí zumbadorcito

chicken
de gallina

emu
de emú

reptile eggs
los huevos de los reptiles

lizard
de lagarto

sea turtle
de tortuga marina

crocodile
de cocodrilo

amphibian eggs
los huevos de los anfibios

newt spawn
desove
de tritón

toad spawn
desove de sapo

surface of the water
la superficie del agua

frog spawn
desove de rana

octopus and squid eggs
los huevos de los pulpos y los calamares

opalescent market squid
de calamar común

veined octopus
de pulpo

fish eggs
los huevos de los peces

salmon
de salmón

lesser spotted dogfish
de pintarroja

sturgeon
de esturión

horn shark
de suño cornudo

mollusk eggs
los huevos de los moluscos

snail
de caracol

insect eggs
los huevos de los insectos

monarch butterfly
de mariposa monarca

spined soldier bug
de chinche común

male carries eggs on its back
el macho lleva los huevos en la espalda

giant water bug
de chinche acuática gigante

ladybug
de vaquita de San Antonio

owl butterfly
de mariposa búho

myriapod eggs
los huevos de los miriápodos

red-headed centipede
de escolopendra roja

arachnid eggs
los huevos de los arácnidos

European garden spider
de araña de jardín europea

silk
la seda

egg sac
la bolsa de huevos

47

Incredible bodies
Cuerpos increíbles

Look at all the parts that make up these amazing animals.

Fíjate en las partes del cuerpo de estos fascinantes animales.

skeletons
los esqueletos

skeleton
el esqueleto

muscles
los músculos

**exoskeleton
(muscles inside
the skeleton)**
el exoesqueleto
(los músculos, dentro
del esqueleto)

muscles
los músculos

bones
los huesos

**endoskeleton
(muscles outside
the skeleton)**
el endoesqueleto
(los músculos, fuera
del esqueleto)

paws
las zarpas

claws
las garras

talons
las garras

**hands
and feet**
**las manos
y los pies**

hoof
la pezuña

fingers
los dedos de
la mano

hand
la mano

toes
los dedos de
los pies

foot
el pie

fin
la aleta
dorsal

flippers
las aletas

**limbs and
appendages**
**las extremidades
y los apéndices**

arms
los brazos

legs
las piernas

tentacles
los tentáculos

48

mane
la melena

scales
las escamas

fur
el pelaje

skin
la piel

bristles
las cerdas

hair
el pelo

wool
la lana

on the body
en el cuerpo

spines
las púas

bill
el pico

eye
el ojo

beak
el pico

tails
las colas

whiskers
los bigotes

ear
el oído

antlers
las astas

heads
las cabezas

membrane
la membrana

tusks
los colmillos

wings
las alas

antennae
las antenas

feather
las plumas

veins
las venas

teeth
los dientes

horns
los cuernos

Defending
Defenderse

Animals have lots of different ways to protect themselves.
Los animales tienen muchas formas distintas de protegerse.

hornet
el avispón

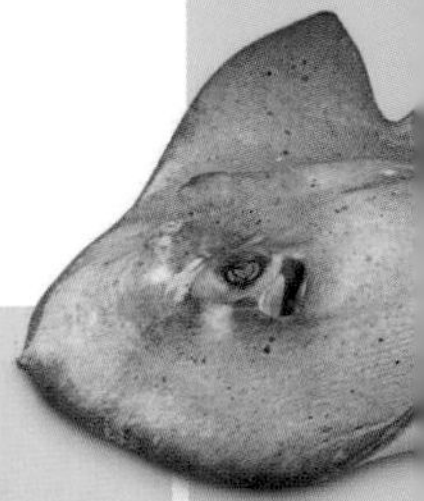

crown of thorns starfish
la corona de espinas

porcupine
el puercoespín

millepede
el milpiés

ball python
la pitón real

hedgehog
el erizo

spikes
las púas

curling up
enroscarse

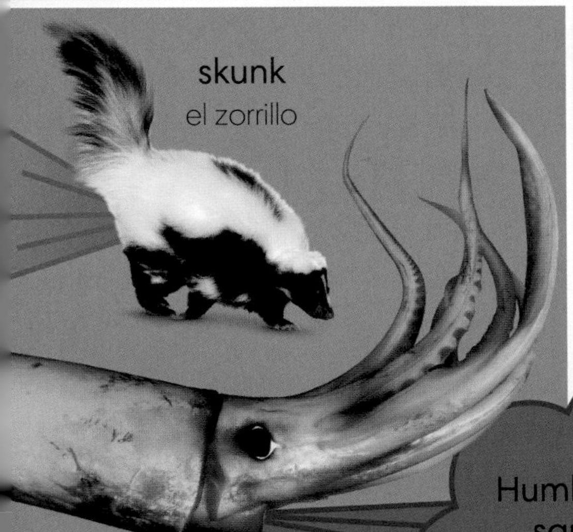

skunk
el zorrillo

crested gecko
el gecko crestado

Humboldt squid
el calamar de Humboldt

opossum
la zarigüella

stone crab
el cangrejo piedra

spraying or squirting
rociar o mojar

playing dead
hacerse el muerto

dropping a limb or tail
desprenderse de una extremidad o la cola

Portuguese man-of-war jellyfish
la carabela portuguesa

whiptail stingray
la raya látigo

bullet ant
la hormiga bala

striped bark scorpion
el escorpión rayado de la corteza

sting
el aguijón

tastes bad
tiene mal sabor

tiger moth
la polilla tigre

fire salamander
la salamandra común

golden frog
la rana dorada

poisonous
los venenosos

Cuban solenodon
el almiquí de Cuba

black mamba
la mamba negra

dangerous
peligrosa

venomous bite
la mordedura venenosa

protection
protección

stings
pica

boxer crab
el cangrejo boxeador

holds an anemone
se agarra a una anémona

using another animal
utilizar otro animal

starlings
los estorninos

school of fish
el banco de peces

meerkat
las suricatas

gathering in groups
reunirse en grupos

armadillo
el armadillo

tortoise beetle
el Cassidinae

Indian pangolin
el pangolín indio

armor plates
las placas de armadura

51

Carnivores and herbivores
Los carnívoros y los herbívoros

Carnivores eat other animals. Herbivores only eat plants. Omnivores have adapted to eat both meat and plants.

Los carnívoros comen otros animales. Los herbívoros solo comen plantas. Los omnívoros están adaptados para comer tanto carne como plantas.

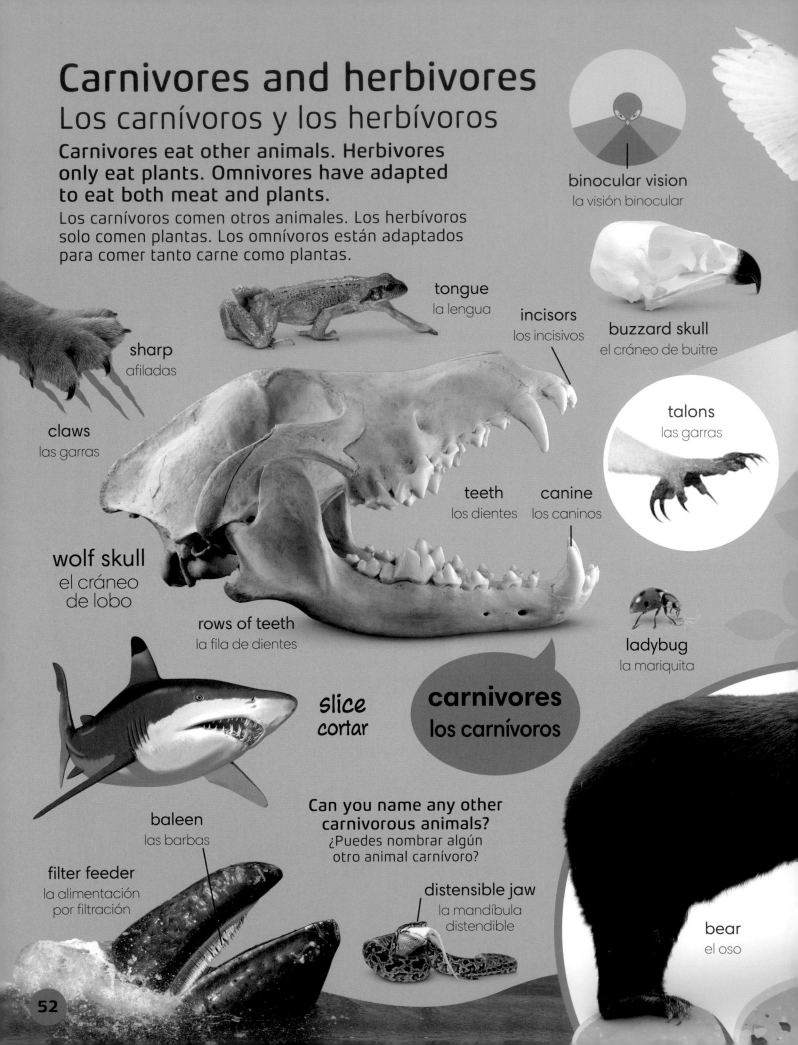

binocular vision
la visión binocular

buzzard skull
el cráneo de buitre

tongue
la lengua

incisors
los incisivos

sharp
afiladas

talons
las garras

claws
las garras

teeth
los dientes

canine
los caninos

wolf skull
el cráneo
de lobo

rows of teeth
la fila de dientes

ladybug
la mariquita

slice
cortar

**carnivores
los carnívoros**

baleen
las barbas

Can you name any other carnivorous animals?
¿Puedes nombrar algún otro animal carnívoro?

filter feeder
la alimentación
por filtración

distensible jaw
la mandíbula
distendible

bear
el oso

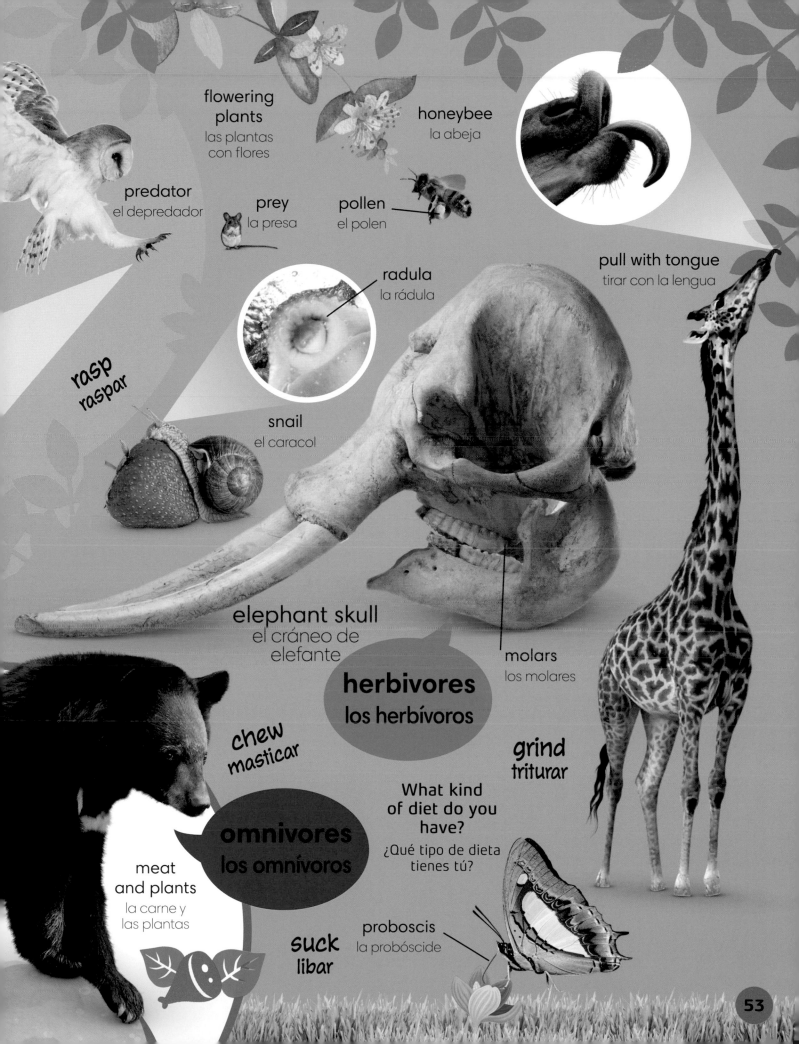

flowering plants
las plantas con flores

honeybee
la abeja

predator
el depredador

prey
la presa

pollen
el polen

pull with tongue
tirar con la lengua

radula
la rádula

rasp
raspar

snail
el caracol

elephant skull
el cráneo de elefante

molars
los molares

herbivores
los herbívoros

chew
masticar

grind
triturar

What kind of diet do you have?
¿Qué tipo de dieta tienes tú?

omnivores
los omnívoros

meat and plants
la carne y las plantas

suck
libar

proboscis
la probóscide

Animal diaries
Los horarios de los animales

Discover what animals get up to at different times of the day and night.

Descubre qué hacen los animales en diferentes momentos del día y de la noche.

tiger el tigre

sleeps in the shade
duerme en la sombra

snoozes
dormita

iguana la iguana

diurnal (active in the day)
diurna (activa de día)

basks to warm up
toma el sol para calentarse

feeds on leaves and fruit
come hojas y frutos

protects territory
protege el territorio

barn owl la lechuza

hunts
caza

sleeps
duerme

dawn
el amanecer

crepuscular (active at dawn and dusk)
crepuscular (activo al amanecer y al anochecer)

morning
la mañana

afternoon
la tarde

nocturnal
(active at night)
nocturno
(activo de noche)

patrols territory
patrulla el territorio

scent marking
marca con su olor

hunts
caza

escapes from
predators
escapa de los depredadores

inactive because
it is colder
inactivo porque hace frío

finds a spot
to rest
busca un
lugar para
descansar

roosts in trees
or empty buildings
se refugia en árboles o en
edificios deshabitados

feeds
come

dusk
el anochecer

evening
el anochecer

night
la noche

People and animals
Las personas y los animales

There are many careers that involve working with animals.

Hay muchas profesiones en las que se trabaja con los animales.

zookeeper
el cuidador del zoológico

wildlife ranger
el guardaparques

zoologist
la zóologa

zoo
el zoológico

horse trainer
el entrenador de caballos

research
investigar

marine biologist
la bióloga marina

camera person
la camarógrafa

study
estudiar

wildlife reporter
la reportera de naturaleza

photographer
la fotógrafa

naturalist
la naturalista

entomologist
el entomólogo

bacteria
las bacterias

camera
la cámara

Would you like to work with animals when you grow up?

¿Te gustaría trabajar con animales cuando seas mayor?

operate
operar

vaccinate
vacunar

jockey
el jinete

groom
la preparadora

rescue
rescatar

rehabilitate
rehabilitar

vet
el veterinario

veterinary nurse
el enfermero veterinario

animal welfare officer
la responsable de salud animal

dog groomer
el peluquero canino

virus
los virus

virologist
la viróloga

dog trainer
el entrenador canino

feed
el forraje

microbiologist
el microbiólogo

beekeeper
el apicultor

honeycomb
el panal

hive
la colmena

farmer
el granjero

Endangered or at risk
Amenazados o en peligro

These animals are badly affected by human activities.
Unless people try to help, they could become extinct.
La actividad humana afecta enormemente a estos animales.
Si no los ayudamos, podrían extinguirse.

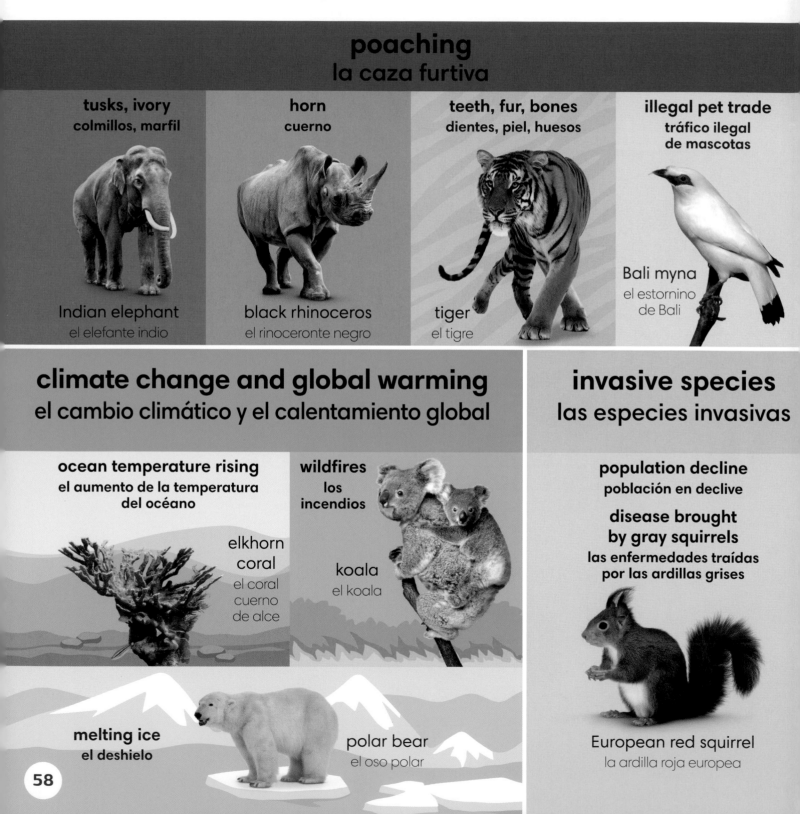

poaching
la caza furtiva

tusks, ivory
colmillos, marfil

Indian elephant
el elefante indio

horn
cuerno

black rhinoceros
el rinoceronte negro

teeth, fur, bones
dientes, piel, huesos

tiger
el tigre

illegal pet trade
tráfico ilegal
de mascotas

Bali myna
el estornino
de Bali

climate change and global warming
el cambio climático y el calentamiento global

invasive species
las especies invasivas

ocean temperature rising
el aumento de la temperatura
del océano

elkhorn
coral
el coral
cuerno
de alce

wildfires
los
incendios

koala
el koala

population decline
población en declive

**disease brought
by gray squirrels**
las enfermedades traídas
por las ardillas grises

melting ice
el deshielo

polar bear
el oso polar

European red squirrel
la ardilla roja europea

disease
la enfermedad

African
wild dog
el licaón
del Cabo

habitat loss
la pérdida del hábitat

**more buildings
for humans**
más edificios
para los humanos

**less habitat
for wildlife**
menos hábitats
para la fauna

urban sprawl
la expansión urbana

Lange's metalmark
butterfly
la mariposa de Lange

Florida panther
la pantera de Florida

loggerhead sea turtle
la tortuga boba

deforestation
la deforestación

**cutting down
trees**
la tala de árboles

orangutan
el orangután

mountain
gorilla
el gorila de
montaña

Canadian caribou
el caribú canadiense

gulf sturgeon
el esturión

fewer bodies of water
menos masas de agua

overhunting and
overfishing
exceso de caza
y sobrepesca

loss of food
pérdida de alimento

Adélie
penguin
el pingüino
de Adelia

Atlantic bluefin tuna
el atún rojo del Atlántico

green sea turtle
la tortuga verde

insecticides
los insecticidas

**chemicals can
kill animals
or make
them sick**
las sustancias
químicas pueden
matar o enfermar
a los animales

San Joaquin
kit fox
la zorrita del
desierto

Crotch's
bumblebee
el abejorro de
Crotch

Extinct species
Las especies extintas

Some animals are unable to adapt as their environment changes, and they become extinct. This means the species has no living members.

Algunos animales son incapaces de adaptarse a los cambios de su entorno y se extinguen. Esto significa que ya no quedan miembros vivos de su especie.

sea scorpions
los escorpiones marinos

spinosaurus
el *Spinosaurus*

giant wombat
el wómbat gigante

saber-toothed tiger
el tigre dientes de sable

Humans often cause the environmental changes that lead to animal extinction.
El ser humano suele causar los cambios ambientales que conducen a la extinción de los animales.

dodo
el dodo

auroch
el *Bos primigenius*

Tasmanian tiger
el tigre de Tasmania

Rocky Mountain locust
la langosta de las Montañas Rocosas

crescent nail-tailed wallaby
el canguro rabipelado occidental

passenger pigeon
la paloma migratoria

Xerces blue Butterfly
el Xerces azul

pig-footed bandicoot
el bandicut de pies de cerdo

Polynesian tree snail
el *Partula nodosa*

New Zealand grayling
el *Prototroctes oxyrhynchus*

brachiosaurus
el *Brachiosaurus*

pteranodon
el *Pteranodon*

iguanodon
el *Iguanodon*

ankylosaurus
el *Ankylosaurus*

allosaurus
el *Allosaurus*

Dinosaurs may have become extinct when a meteorite collided with the Earth.
Los dinosaurios podrían haberse extinguido cuando un meteorito chocó contra la Tierra.

woolly mammoth
el mamut lanudo

Eastern elk
el uapití

great auk
el alca gigante

Caribbean monk seal
la foca monje del Caribe

Steller's sea cow
la vaca marina de Steller

Pyrenean ibex
el bucardo

West African black rhinoceros
el rinoceronte negro occidental

millions of years ago
hace millones de años

tens of thousands of years ago
hace decenas de miles de años

recent history
historia reciente

Mythical creatures
Las criaturas míticas

Some animals exist only in stories. Every culture has its own stories and its own mythical beasts.

Algunos animales solo existen en los cuentos. Todas las culturas tienen sus historias y sus propios animales míticos.

faun
el fauno

Hydra
la hidra

fairy
el hada

Pegasus
el pegaso

werewolf
el hombre lobo

bigfoot
Pie Grande

Kun-Peng
el Kun-Peng

centaur
el centauro

leprechaun
el *leprechaun*

Cerberus
Cerbero

dragon
el dragón

Jiuwei Hu
Huli jing

Zouwu
Zouyu

Chinese dragon
el dragón chino

mermaid
la sirena

manticore
la mantícora

Which of these mythical creatures do you recognize?
¿Cuáles de estas criaturas míticas reconoces?

unicorn
el unicornio

sphinx
la esfinge

kraken
el kraken

troll
el trol

Ao
Ao

elf
el elfo

Pixiu
Pixiu

minotaur
el minotauro

chi
el chi

griffin
el grifo

phoenix
el fénix

Harpy
la harpía

Loch Ness Monster
el monstruo del lago Ness

Shang-Yang
Shang Yang

yeti
el yeti

Acknowledgments

Agradecimientos

Dorling Kindersley would like to thank Sif Nørskov and Sophie Parkes for editorial assistance, Polly Goodman for proofreading, and Jane Perlmutter for Americanizing.

The publisher would like to thank the following for their kind permission to reproduce their photographs:
(Key: a-above; b-below/bottom; c-center; f-far; l-left; r-right; t-top)

123RF.com: Andrzej Tokarski / ajt 64br, Anan Kaewkhammul / anankkml 28ca, Benjamin King / benjaminjk 51ca, bonzami emmanuelle 20c, Corey A Ford 61tc, Duncan Noakes / fouroaks 17ca, Eric Isselee 7cb, 50cl, 50clb, Eric Isselee / isselee 1bl, 28cr, 29cra, 58cb, Anan Kaewkhammul 28cl, max5128 16cra, Ben McRae 41cla (texture), nrey 2tr, Andrei Samkov / satirus 52c, smileus 44bl, swavo 6cra (glass), 11cl (glass), 32cla (glass), Thawat Tanhai 38clb (Kingfisher), Nicholas Toh 37bl, Pavlo Vakhrushev / vapi 9cb, 64crb, Oleg Znamenskiy zov666@gmail.com 41ca; **Alamy Stock Photo:** AGAMI Photo Agency / Andy & Gill Swash 40bc, Linda Freshwaters Arndt 34cla, Art Collection 3 60crb (wallaby), Avalon.red / Anthony Bannister 11cr, Avalon.red / Stephen Dalton 35tc, Biosphoto / Adam Fletcher 39cla, Biosphoto / Sergio Hanquet 51clb, Biosphoto / Sylvain Cordier 42ca (nest), blickwinkel / AGAMI / J. Eaton 36cla, blickwinkel / F. Hecker 42c, 45bc, blickwinkel / F. Teigler 11bc, blickwinkel / H. Bellmann / F. Hecker 45br, blickwinkel / Lundqvist 40clb, Buiten-Beeld / Jelger Herder 14clb, Nigel Cattlin 11ca, cbstockfoto 43cb, Clarence Holmes Wildlife 47clb, Corbin17 38bl, Rick Dalton - Wildlife 59ca, Design Pics Inc / Alaska Stock RM / Thomas Kline 47cl, Digital Arts Pro 48cr, Reinhard Dirscherl 37c, 39bc, David Fleetham 20crb (puffer), 51cr, Florilegius 60crb (bandicoot), FLPA 26cb (Elkhound), 47tr, 61crb, Bill Gozansky 40bl, Frank Hecker 21clb, Louise Heusinkveld 54bc (sleep), Imagebroker / Arco / G. Lacz 29crb, imageBROKER / Dirk Funhoff 15ca, imageBROKER / Gerry Pearce 17c, 33c, imageBROKER / Michaela Walch 43tr, imageBROKER / R. Dirscherl 36bl, Juniors Bildarchiv GmbH / Arndt, S.E. / juniors@wildlife 55bc, Ivan Kuzmin 10bl, mike lane 19br, M@rcel 43br, Francisco Martinez-Clavel Martinez 10c, Chris Mattison 41cb, mauritius images GmbH / BY 25c, mauritius images GmbH / Solvin Zankl 46bc, McPhoto / Rolf Mueller 17tr, Mic Clark Photography 55cra, Minden Pictures / Norbert Wu 20bl, 47ca (horn), Natural History Museum, London 60clb, 61cb, Nature Photographers Ltd / Paul R. Sterry 8clb (Shrimp), 20br, 32clb, 43bc (moth), 47tc, Nature Picture Library 31cl, 50bl, Nature Picture Library / 2020VISION / Alex Mustard 21c, Nature Picture Library / Bence Mate 32crb, Nature Picture Library / Chris Mattison 15cra, Nature Picture Library / Eric Medard 42cla, Nature Picture Library / MYN / Joris van Alphen 15c, Nature Picture Library / MYN / Lily Kumpe 10cr, Nature Picture Library / MYN / Marc Pihet 43fclb, Nature Picture Library / Nick Upton 42bc, Andrey Nekrasov 16br, NOAA 37cl, Matteo Omied 59tr, Panoramic Images 49bc, Papilio / Robert Pickett 47crb (Owl), PhotoStock-Israel / Alon Meir 44cl, Picture Partners 47ca, Adisha Pramod 37cr, 37clb, Gillian Pullinger 42bc (warren), Lee Rentz 14cl, Remo Savisaar 42bl, SBS Eclectic Images 18bl, Robert Scholl 22bl, steeve-x-art 60bl, Marko Steffensen 37crb, Stefan Sutka 28bl, Tom K Photo 58cl, Dave Watts 18ca, WhiskeyWolf 61br, WILDLIFE GmbH 21crb, Ray Wilson 12ca (albatross); **Ardea:** Danita Delimont / Kevin Schafer 48br, M. Watson 45cla; **J. Buys:** 47bl; **Depositphotos Inc:** DedMorozz 54ca, Nataly-Nete 35ca (Grass), sophyphotos 6bc; **Dorling Kindersley:** Jerry Young 8clb, 64tl, Gary Ombler / Cotswold Wildlife Park 17cla, Neil Fletcher 43fcrb, Terry Goss 21bl, Brian Gratwicke 32crb (eel), Jon Hughes 61cla, Barnabas Kindersley 49fbl, Liberty's Owl, Raptor and Reptile Centre, Hampshire, UK 40ca, Richard Ling 9tl, Prof. Marcio Motta 28cla, Colin Keates / Natural History Museum, London 40tc, 46br, 49bl, Frank Greenaway / Natural History Museum, London 8c, 51tr, 54bc, Gary Ombler / Natural History Museum 29bl, Karl Shone / Natural History Museum, London 23cl, Peter Chadwick / Natural History Museum, London 52cra, Linda Pitkin 41tr, Gary Ombler / Royal Botanic Gardens, Kew 64br (leaves), Harry Taylor The Natural History Museum, London 6bl, Dave King / Whipsnade Zoo, Bedfordshire 17tr (bear), Wildlife Heritage Foundation, Kent, UK 29clb, Jerry Young 2bl, 10clb, 17bc, 38ca, 39br; **Dreamstime.com:** 3drenderings 8clb (woodlouse), Adchariya 43fbl, Anastasiya Aheyeva 42cb (otter), Alfotokunst 17crb, Alle 57cb, 57bc, Alptraum 15bl, Alslutsky 56bc, Carlos Alvarez 27clb, Alxhar 48cla, Amwu 1cl, 25tl, 35crb, Anders93 47crb, John Anderson 58clb, Andylid 24clb, Amy Harris / Anharris 53r, Anitasstudio 53cl, Rafael Ben Ari 36crb, Andrey Armyagov 7br, Atalvi 31cla, Bouke Atema 13crb, Auris 36-37, Natalia Bachkova 35clb, Jason W. Baker 10crb, Belizar 51cb (Amradillo), Christopher Bellette 6cra (spider), Ben 38cb, John Biglin 42br, Lukas Blazek 29ca, Blueringmedia 35c (branch), 63cla, Anna Bocharova 25tc, Linda Bucklin 1br, 16b, 60crb, Mariusz Bugno 12cla, Neil Burton 35tc (hare), Steve Byland 7tc, 12br, 13bc, Martin Capek / Cappan 32crb (lighting), Carolinemaryan 24cra, Vladimir Cech 18cla, Chernetskaya 25br (tray), Chuotnhatdesigner 34-35b, Conchasdiver 36fbl, Rudmer Zwerver / Creativenature1 14bc, Brett Critchley 48cb, 49c, Cynoclub 11cra, Damedeeso 35br, Olga Demchishina 33bl, Nikolay Denisov 36tr, Dikkyoesin 39tr, Dave Massey / Dmass 53ca, Dndavis 39ca, Dennis Donohue 12cra, Dragoneye 13cla, 38fcra, Dwiputra18 39cb, Ian Dyball 33tl, Ecophoto 19cr, Dirk Ercken 15clb, 25cl, Evcrow 35b, Farinoza 24crb, 36clb, 39cb (frog), 49ca (spines), Melinda Fawver 39clb (Moth), Feathercollector 41cra, Ricardo De Paula Ferreira 43tc (Rufous), Iakov Filimonov 26cra, 40br, Fireflamenco 2fbl, 63cr, Svetlana Foote 32cr, 58c, Corey A Ford 60c, FotoJagodka 26clb, Martin Fredskov 42cb, Robert Fullerton 40cla, Gallinagomedia 12crb, Svetlana Gladkova 54cl, Godruma 42fbr, Steve Gould 6crb, Igor Groshev 42cr, Pascal Halder 33r, David Havel 39bc (anemone), 41br, Hellmann1 56l (Bark), Nynke Van Holten 29cr, Brett Hondow 35cl, Hsagencia 35bc (worm), Boonchuay Iamsumang 34cr, Icefront 13clb, Idreamphotos 45tl, Imagine98 49crb (whiskers), Inarik 34c, Irisbraunphotography 44crb, Eric Isselee 27ca (collie), Isselee 1ca, 8cr, 11cb, 12cr, 13ca, 13cl, 13c, 13cb (tit), 13bl, 13br, 14br, 17crb (koala), 18ca (tamarin), 19tc, 20cra, 20crb (Clownfish), 22c, 23tr, 23b, 24bl, 24bc, 25tc (gecko), 25cr, 26bl, 27tc, 27tr, 27cra, 27cb, 27bc, 29tc, 29cla, 30cb, 31tr, 31cr, 31clb, 34cl, 34bc, 35tl, 39cra, 39clb, 40tr, 40cb, 42cra (boar), 42clb, 42bl (Rabbit), 42fbl, 44cb (fawn), 45tc, 45ca, 45clb (x2), 45cb, 45bl, 49ca, 49cb (deer), 49cb (fly), 54-55ca, 55clb, 56cl, 58br, Maria Itina 19cl, Iakov Filimonov / Jackf 59c, JaCrispy 24cla, Jacsdreamjam 46bl, Jagodka 27br, James Group Studios, Inc. 25bl (cage), Jeff Jarrett 43clb, Jessamine 1crb, Jezbennett 19tc (Lemur), Jianghongyan 9tc, Jocrebbin 52b, Johannes Gerhardus Swanepoel / Johan63 41tc, Johannesk 35crb (Sand), 38crb, Angela Jones 35cb, Josefpittner 40cla (fox), Juliengrondin 54br, 55cb (Oak), Acharaporn Kamornboonyarush 10bc, Karelgallas 52-53bc, John Kasawa 34-35cb, Kateleigh 30crb, Elena Kazanskaya 25bl (bell), Alexia Khruscheva 49tr, Khunaspix 31crb, Liliia Khuzhakhmetova 16ca, Miroslaw Kijewski 40clb (mantis), Aleksei Kondraiuk 34bl, Natalia Korotaeva 32br, Vasily Kovalev 25fcr, Irina Kozhemyakina 10cb (x2), 17cl, Anna Kravchuk 34clb (Sandpiper), Tomas Krist 34cra, Matthijs Kuijpers 24tr, 39tl, 51c, Olga Kurbatova 57b, Alexey Kuznetsov 26ca, Erik Lam 27ca, 27bl, Lebedinski 26cb, Peter Lindholm 6c (Crayfish), Liumangtiger 13clb (macaw), Luayana 40br (texture), Thomas Lukassek 43c (limpet), Lunamarina 18cl, 20cb, Tono Balaguer / Lunamarina 59clb, Anton Lunkov 50cla, Yurii Lysiak 23cr, Macrovector 62tr, 62ca, 62c, 62cr, 62bl, 63 (x6), 63cb, 63cb (Minotaur), Cosmin Manci 10cl, Marcouliana 10ca, Marish 63clb, Marquise132 47cr, Martinlisner 20crb, Sutisa Kangvansap / Mathisa 53cb, Vaclav Matous 16crb, Aliaksandr Mazurkevich 19bl, Mikelane45 12c, 13cr, 18cb, 42cl, 42br (vole), 51cb, Ekaterina Mikhailova 61tr, Mirek1967 43cra, Mirkorosenau 38cra, Mouse Family Mouse Family 25br, Natalya Aksenova / Natalyaa 31cb (duck), Pavel Naumov 53bc, Sivakorn Nayanetra 31bl, Neirfy 30clb, 31br, Yin Jian Ng 35bc, Nivanova250788 62cl (bigfoot), Duncan Noakes 16cr, Nostradamus252 34br, Rungroj Nuiman 43br (Antx2), Nyker 16c, Nylakatara2013 42ca, Veronika Oliinyk 1clb, Olga Itina / Olikit 35tr, Onyxprj 63cr (elf), Eline Oostingh 18bc, Ornitolog 12ca, Oskanov 43tc, Oxilixo 31bc, Paleka 50c, Kevin Panizza / Kpanizza 9bl, Juan Bautista Ruiz Páramo 43ca, Parfentevamaya 21cla, Dmytro Parkheta 43cl, Gueret Pascale 59crb, Prosun Paul 11tl, Maksim Pauliukevich 34cla (dust), 35ca (dust), Kostya Pazyuk 25c (rabbit), Peerapong Peattayakul 24ca, Martin Pelanek 43cr, Azahara Perez 61clb, Stefan Hermans / Perrush 49cla, Photoclarity 25bl, Photoeuphoria 41cr, Pimmimemom 47clb (Monarch), Peter Leahy / Pipehorse 59cra, Elena Podolnaya 42crb, Stu Porter 12bl, Alexander Potapov 31cb, Grobler Du Preez 43tl, Ondřej Prosický 19ca, 38cla, 40cra, 59tl, Pytyczech 1tc, 56br, Rogerio Queiroz 43tc (nest), Alexander Raths 20cr, Mohd Zaidi Abdul Razak 39tc, Ian Redding 47tl, Rhallam 30cra, Francesco Ricciardi 6br, 39c, Dan Rieck 59cb, Rikke68 3cb, 34tr, Rinus Baak / Rinusbaak 32ca, 38ca (Macaw), Eurico Rodrigues 39bl, Craig Russell 43crb, Kaewmanee Saekang 7clb, Samum 49fcla, Sarah2 8crb, Seaonweb 38br, Anna Sedneva / Sedneva 53b, Inha Semiankova 24ca (pond), Yury Shirokov 31bc (Cat), Pavel Shlykov 27clb (Russell), Andrei Shupilo 8cla, 8cl, Slowmotiongli 7crb, 13cb, 19tl, 35ca, 47cb, 51tl, 55cla, Simone Gatterwe / Smgirly 30bl, Smileus 22br, Michael G Smith 6cla, Olya Solodenko 24cra (bed), David Steele 43ftl, Andreas Steidlinger 43bl, Studio 37 / Dreamstock 38cr, Stu Porter / Stuporter 29tl, Kedsirin Suthamsakul 51crb, Tartilastock 34clb (trees), Taviphoto 12bc (duck), Thawats 34tr (monarch), 34cra (flutter), Charoenchai Tothaisong 55cl, Trinhhuytho 35bl, Troichenko 11c, Sergey Uryadnikov 17cr, 19bc, Vac 17br, Veleknez 31c, Venturebeyond 47tc (Squid), Verastuchelova 24br, 49cl, Gale Verhague 10br, Vasiliy Vishnevskiy 49cla (Rat), Viter8 30br, Vaclav Vitovec 10cla, Vladvitek 12bc, 21tc, 39cl, Yehor Vlasenko 2br, 62-63bc, Tomislav Vucic 43c, Wafuefotodesign 49cb, Wahyudinfirman 52bc, Gary Webber 40tr (texture), Welcomia 59bc, Ashley Whitworth 7cra, Buddee Wiangngorn 9cla, 9bl (sand), 37b, Apisit Wilaijit 41clb, Wildlife World 13cb (sparrow), Jan Martin Will 59cl, William Wise 50cb, Marcin Wojciechowski 1cb, Wollertz 34clb, Jinfeng Zhang 11cla, Katerina Zmachynska 63cla (ship), Rudmer Zwerver 15crb, 17tc, 34clb (Kingfisher), 53cla; **Fotolia:** anankkml 55ca, giuliano2022 6cl, Eric Isselee 44br, Sergey Khachatryan 49br, Andrey Eremin / mbongo 47tl (Waves), xstockerx 64tr, Stefan Zeitz / Lux 12cl; **Getty Images:** Collection Mix: Subjects / Michael Nolan 37tr, Brandon Tabiolo / Design Pics 6cb, Sylke Rohrlach / EyeEm 37cb (slug), imageBROKER / Reinhold Schrank 43bc, Moment / Stan Tekiela Author / Naturalist / Wildlife Photographer 36cra, Moment / Tambako the Jaguar 48ca, Stone / Michael Duva 35cr, Westend61 21br; **Getty Images / iStock:** 2630ben 17tl, alkir 22cra, Andyworks 28bc, Antagain 1tl, 31crb (bees), Aunt_Spray 60tr, Kristian Baensch 44cla, BionicPanda 63br, Boyshots 44bl (wombat), Vicky_Chauhan 51br, CoreyFord 44ca, defun 22cb, dennisvdw 19tr, sserg_dibrova 36-37bc, DigitalVision Vectors / exxorian 62br, E+ / 4FR 53tr, E+ / Kativ 47br, E+ / KenCanning 16cla, 44clb, E+ / Raycat 56crb, E+ / vusta 23crb, Entwicklungsknecht 35c, feedough 52cla, Liliya Filakhtova 10cl (beetle), Flexire 39crb, FrankRamspott 50ca, girlfrommars 62cb, GlobalP 31tl, 31ca, 41cla, Grisha459 55cr, Taisiia Iaremchuk 63tl, Kaphoto 30cr, KeithSzafranski 44tr, Piotr Krzeslak 30bc, Lanaclipart 62cla, leonello 61cra, lillybell 44bc, Lidiia Lykova 44cb, micro_photo 57cl, mtruchon 30ca, Hachio Nora 62cl, Placebo365 43cla, proxyminder 56l, reptiles4all 22cb (terrapin), Chelsea Sampson 38clb, Victoria Shapkina 63bc, Sieboldianus 55cb, 55crb, Christophe Sirabella 20clb, stanley45 22cla, studiocasper 48clb, SurfUpVector 62crb, Tazzy1 29bc, undefined 18crb, vendys 35fcrb; **naturepl.com:** Philip Dalton 37cla, Georgette Douwma 36bc, 37br, Tim Laman 37ca, Thomas Marent 28cra, 36c, Alex Mustard 36br (limpet), 37bc, MYN / Brett Lewis 15cb, Piotr Naskrecki 37tl, Nature Production 37cra, Gary Bell / Oceanwide 32bc, Pete Oxford 36br, Morley Read 15br, Andy Sands 32tr, David Shale 36bc (sponge), 37cb, Nick Upton 42c (holt), Doug Wechsler 14ca, Rod Williams 28clb, Solvin Zankl 32bl; **Science Photo Library:** Mauricio Anton 60cla, Nicholas Bergkessel, Jr. 35cla, British Antarctic Survey 36cb, Robert Chase 61cb (seal), Dennis Kunkel Microscopy 6cra, K Jayaram 37ca (frog), Andrew J. Martinez 50br, Cordelia Molloy 29br, Nicholas Smythe 36ca, Roman Uchytel 60cl, 61cl; **Shutterstock.com:** Kurit afshen 55c, Dray van Beeck 39cr, Billion Photos 24cb, Jude Black 10tr, BRO.vector 63bc (harpy), Cingular 6cr, Jesus Cobaleda 39bl (parrotfish), 50-51ca, delcarmat 62bc, Dirk Ercken 1cra, Erni 16cl, Gerald Robert Fischer 49crb, Gallinago_media 48c, Anton Kozyrev 10cra, MongPro 48cra, Mr.Photomato 42cra, NickEvansKZN 23tl, panpilai paipa 24cla (fish), RealityImages 41crb, Porco_Rosso 59br, Sarah2 11cl, sonelle.vdm 43tc (Weaver), I Wayan Sumatika 60br, Pavaphon Supanantananont 38br (basslet), vkilikov 20cl, Wirestock Creators 11bl, Michiel de Wit 14cr, chonlasub woravichan 38bc, xpixel 25tr, Milan Zygmunt 54c; **SuperStock:** Biosphoto / Gregory Guida 46cb, Science Photo Library 6c; **Didier Descouens, Museum of Toulouse:** 46cr

Cover images: *Front:* **123RF.com:** Thawat Tanhai (Kingfisher), Pavlo Vakhrushev / vapi (jellyfish); **Dorling Kindersley:** Peter Chadwick / Natural History Museum, London (skull), Gary Ombler / Royal Botanic Gardens, Kew (leaves); **Dreamstime.com:** Isselee (prairie), Jianghongyan (clam), Nyker (Llama), Olga Itina / Olikit (horse), Palex66 (insect), Kevin Panizza / Kpanizza (Sponge), Pytyczech (Morpho), Rinus Baak / Rinusbaak (Bat), Sarah2 (tick), Yobro10 (Elephant), Rudmer Zwerver (Mouse); **Fotolia:** xstockerx (GPig); Front and Back: **123RF.com:** Eric Isselee / isselee (Koala); **Dorling Kindersley:** Jerry Young (Gramma), (tetras), (Spider); **Dreamstime.com:** Veronika Oliinyk (footmarks), Korn Vitthayanukarun (texture), Linda Bucklin (Whale), Farinoza (bushbaby), Irisangel (feather), Isselee (Clownfish), (Cockatoo), Johannesk (Moorish), Dirk Ercken / kikkerdirk (frogx2), Irina Kozhemyakina (opossum), Brian Kushner (Eagle), Alexander Potapov (duck), Rikke68 (Buzzard), Studio 37 / Dreamstock (Redfish), Marcin Wojciechowski (Reindeer); **Fotolia:** Stefan Zeitz / Lux (puffin); **Getty Images / iStock:** anankkml (puma), Antagain (parrot), chris2766 (hen), GlobalP (Axolotl), (fox), Kaphoto (Ant); **Shutterstock.com:** Dirk Ercken (frog); *Back:* **123RF.com:** Eric Isselee / isselee (Koala); **Dorling Kindersley:** Frank Greenaway / Natural History Museum, London (Moth), Robert Royse (Willow); **Dreamstime.com:** Annaav (Fennec), Ben (Peacock), Brad Calkins / Bradcalkins (snail), Linda Bucklin (Whale), Farinoza (bushbaby), Irisangel (feather), Isselee (spider), (Clownfish), (Cockatoo), (Tortoise), Rinus Baak / Rinusbaak (Macaw); Spine: **Dreamstime.com:** Johannesk (Moorish); **Shutterstock.com:** Dirk Ercken (frog)

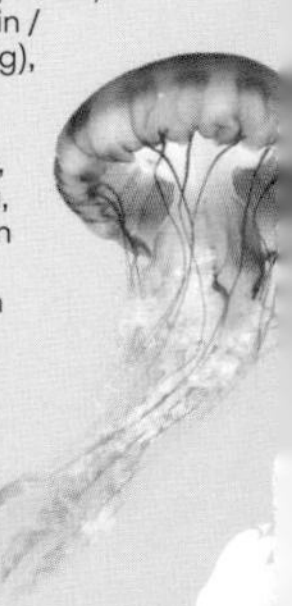